Cartoons from
PUNCH

Edited by William Hewison

 Robson Books

FIRST PUBLISHED IN 1979 BY ROBSON BOOKS LTD.,
28 POLAND STREET, LONDON WIV 3DB. COPYRIGHT
© 1979 PUNCH PUBLICATIONS LIMITED.

British Library Cataloguing in Publication Data

Cartoons from 'Punch'

   1. Caricatures and cartoons – Great Britain
   1. Hewison, William
   2. Punch
   741.5 942   NC1476

First impression October 1979
Second impression November 1980
Third impression August 1983
Fourth impression November 1983
Sixth impression August 1984
Seveth impression July 1985

   ISBN 0-86051-089-1

Printed in Hungary.

Introduction

Cartoonists who regularly send their stuff to *Punch* sometimes
complain that the cartoon accepted from that week's batch is the
"dud" they included at the last moment—a run of the mill make-
weight stuck in just to show they haven't been slacking. The great,
mould-breaking smasheroo, the inspired master-gag they believe will
take its place among the classics of all time—that is the one the
postman slings back on to their front door mat.

This suggests that cartoonists are not the best judges of their own
work. Alternatively, it could mean that the editor and art editor of
Punch are letting a lot of high quality material slip through their
fingers. Well, perhaps. As the man said, we don't always laugh at the
same thing; one man's favourite cartoon is another man's very damp
squib. Even so, I'm prepared to put my neck on the block and claim
that this selection, in its broad sweep from the knockabout through
to the zany and in the variety of its drawing styles, hits the target
again and again. Some of the cartoons are quick-fire, some seek a
little effort from the reader and delay their point, some have double-
takes and resonances that vibrate long after the page has been
turned. Some make a satirical point, some comment on human
frailty and human conceit, some are surreal doodles, some result
from shaking the cartoonists' tricks into a new alignment. One or
two, perhaps, because of their demands on the reader or the
idiosyncrasies of their humour, will not register with everyone.

But don't worry; a cartoon by its very nature is a little riddle that
needs to be solved—it is not a test in which you pass or fail.
Cartoons are there to be enjoyed, and provided you haven't been
locked away in a cellar these last twenty years, I feel sure you will
enjoy this collection.
W.H.

*"When you sold me that weed-killer you
mentioned nothing about possible side-effects!"*

Family Ground

"It sounds like those bloody idiots upstairs are playing their Stockhausen records again."

"Let me get this straight, young man. You seek annulment of the marriage on the grounds that the bride's father didn't have a licence for the gun."

"For Heaven's sake ask him how he's getting on with his body building course."

"If God had meant us to live within our means He wouldn't have given us credit cards!"

"No, no, you're not disturbing us. We were just horsing around listening to Webern, discussing Wittgenstein, and stuff like that."

STANLEY by Murray Ball

Continuing the adventures of the Great Palaeolithic Hero

"*Look, baby! Daddy's making a personal appearance.*"

"*. . . Miss Maureen Lumley?*"

"We seem an awfully long way from a cashpoint."

*"Just wait until **you** want to run barefoot in the meadow!"*

"*Linda and I are getting a divorce, and we divided up our friends. I got you.*"

"*I'm not fussy about the style—I just want something that will get me from A to B.*"

"*I hope you're really ill—you know I don't like making house calls, and for goodness sake stop moaning about how seldom I visit you, mother!*"

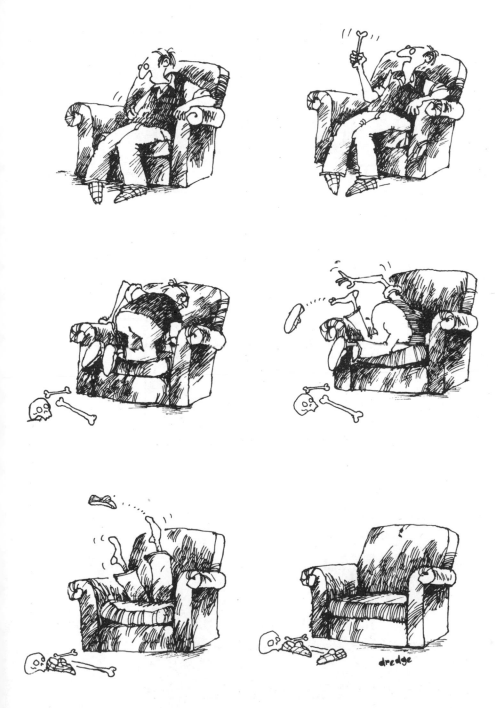

dredge

"We didn't know a damn thing about the right-of-way until after we had the pool put in."

"There goes a car with exactly the same number as ours."

CHILDREN'S LIBRARY

by

Quentin Blake

"*Have you got a book about a little girl who lives in a lovely house and one day a fairy gives her three wishes and all lovely flowers come up all over the garden and she meets a unicorn and she finds a magic box and her Mummy comes and calls her in for tea?*"

STANLEY by Murray Ball

Continuing the adventures of the Great Palaeolithic Hero

"Look—if you have five pocket calculators and I take two away, how many have you got left?"

"I only just made it before my Dad's vasectomy."

"We had Oscar Wilde today, sweetie."

"Have you anything in the way of wholesome family entertainment with innuendo?"

"Now, gang, I want you to go out there and give a performance seldom seen in the theatre today. I want you, Miss Parkman, as Lydia Tarkington the alcoholic wife, to display a rare talent which brings to the part twenty five years experience on Broadway. And you, Angela Dacey, as the kooky secretary, I want you to bear watching as the most promising actress to come along since Blythe Danner. And you, Edmund. . ."

"I don't think it's to do with your begetting an infant prodigy, dad, so much as it's to do with your being stupid."

*"I often say, Mrs. Dent, I'd rather have your little Christopher in my class than **all** the bright, clever ones!"*

"What's a transvestite, mom?"

"Golly, I'm glad you noticed! There's no point in suffering from depression if nobody notices."

"*Best cigarette of the day, I always think . . .*"

ROY DAVIS

*"Permission to move my
cell around, sir?"*

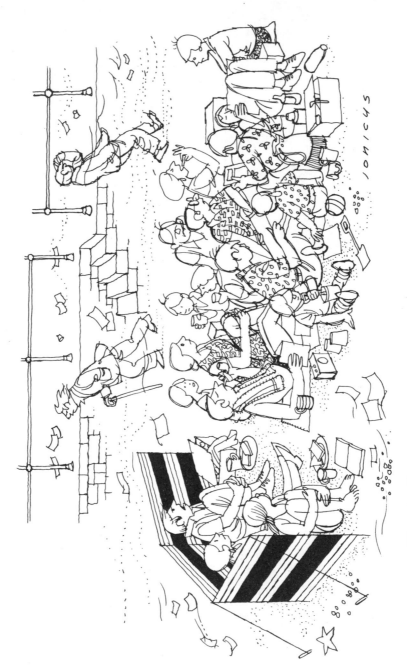

"Parasites!"

"Get a pang of conscience every damn house we crawl past."

"When the flag's up you leave two hundred and eighty-four pints and when it's down you leave two hundred and eighty-three."

"I'm sorry I've kept you waiting, but I see you've made yourself at home."

"You'd think, for the amount we're paying in rates, they'd draw and quarter him as well."

"I get restless in the spring. I wish the council would make us move on."

Dogs and Other Animals

"I'm enrolled at the Kennel-Club—whatever a kennel is . . ."

"Well, wherever he is, he's just dug up two dozen snowdrops!"

STANLEY by Murray Ball

Continuing the adventures of the Great Palaeolithic Hero

"So, once he'd smuggled me through Customs, I thought, what the hell!"

"Why not admit it—you really wanted a budgie."

"*Frankly, I feel he over-disciplines his animals.*"

"*Keeping a friendship in constant repair cuts both ways, you know.*"

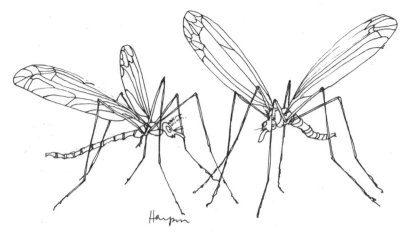

"Can I snuggle up to you?"

*"I'm afraid off the peg's
going to be difficult."*

STANLEY by Murray Ball

Continuing the adventures of the Great Palaeolithic Hero

"Oh, hell! Are you sure? I was hoping we were Lust."

"You're right!
It *is* eating ants!"

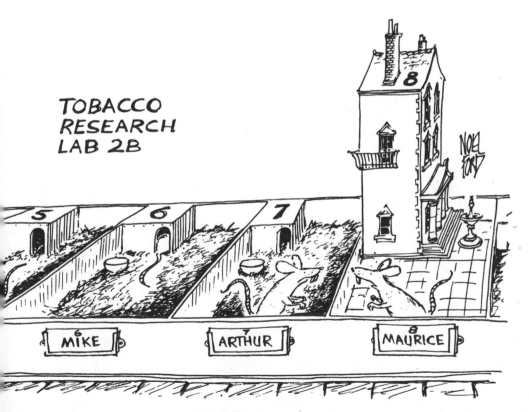

TOBACCO
RESEARCH
LAB 2B

"Pure luck, really—my father was on coupon brands."

HARGREAVES

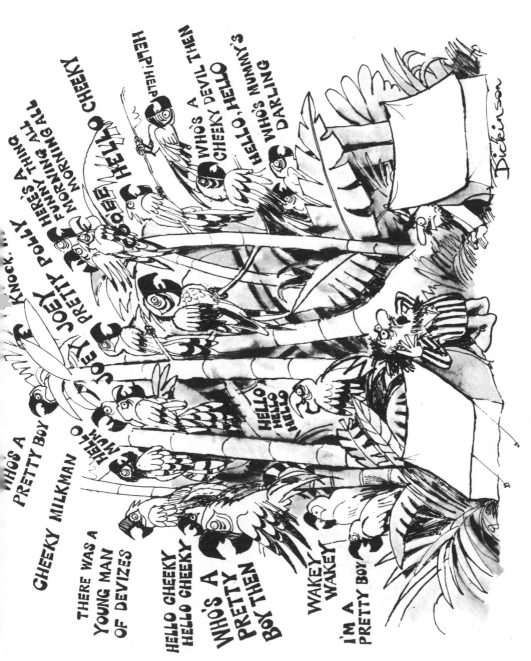

"Blast this flaming dawn chorus!"

"What do you mean, no?"

"Take no notice—he's showing off."

"Stop thief!"

"It has come to my knowledge that in private you refer to me as 'Honky'."

"I think they've spotted the hide, Neville."

Work and Leisure

"I always understood they just shuffled around being mistaken for one of the gardeners."

"*They should get rid of that centre-forward for a start. He's useless.*"

"Phew, that was quite a day."

"And returned by one o'clock. I go to lunch then."

"*You ought to read Marx and Lenin, luv'. They've opened my eyes!*"

"*A man in my position has a sacred duty to foment revolution!*"

"*I'll just nip round and see how our other shop's doing.*"

Hollowood

"I know you said you had no vacancies, but on the phone you sounded as though you thought I might be coloured."

Nick

"Aha! Trying to buy us off with huge salaries and great working conditions, huh?"

"If you can't do better than that, Riley, you'll find yourself on After Sales Service."

"Fred — that black Wolseley with the light on top."

"Enter stage left."

"*You're slow today—I've finished my side and . . .*"

"This is going to make a bloody fantastic four-page, full-colour spread..."

"... graffiti, the new art-form of the underprivileged masses..."

"... the voice of the proletariat screaming its protest from the walls of the decadent capitalists' city strong-hold..."

"Some of you students have urged me to teach that bourgeois society is corrupt, so here goes. Bourgeois society is corrupt. Returning now to the question of congruent triangles . . ."

"Look at that, all over our car, the dirty little bastards!"

STANLEY by Murray Ball

Continuing the adventures of the Great Palaeolithic Hero

"But it's all you ever do—practise Lying in State!"

"It's the same year after year—nobody ever turns up!"

"*You're not really a hypochondriac. You only think you're a hypochondriac.*"

"*I'd like to say I've never received such a complete and thorough overhaul.*"

"I wanted something for a rather more feminine type of man."

"This is treachery—they've stolen our deceptive wording that gets round the Trade Description Act."

"It's your round."

"Where's Gordon?"

"You can tell he's in agriculture. Typical farmers' pallor."

*"So help me, Captain, it was a great white whale
when I first saw it."*

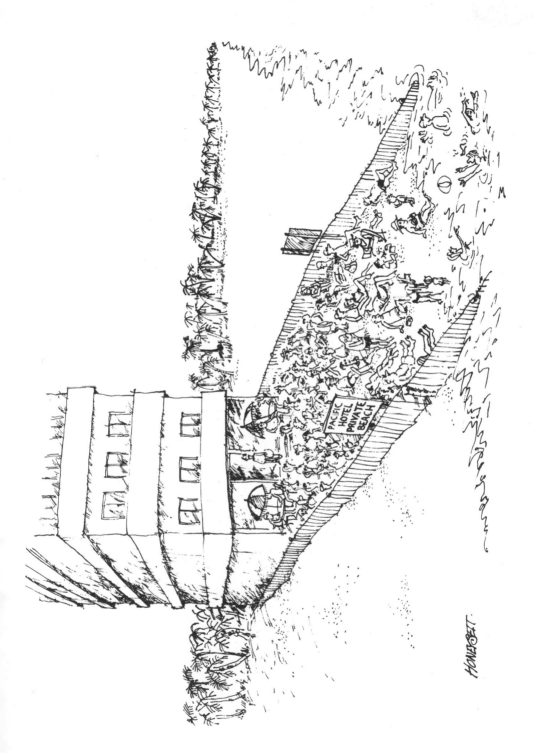

"Hey! Where's my transistor, and who switched it off?"

"It may be art but it's bloody poor welding."

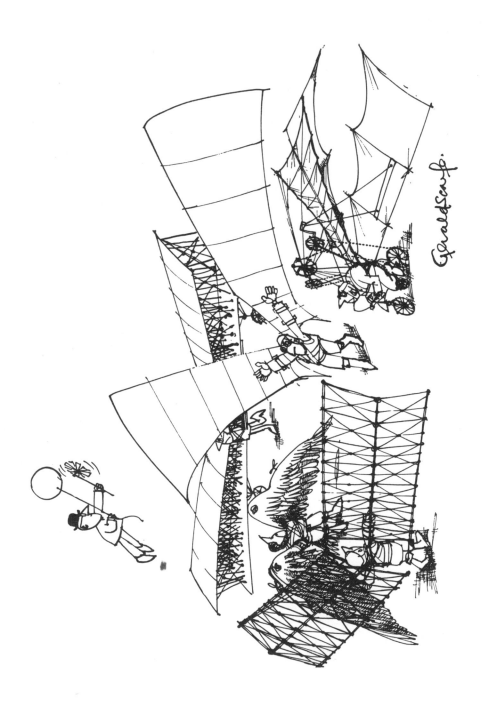

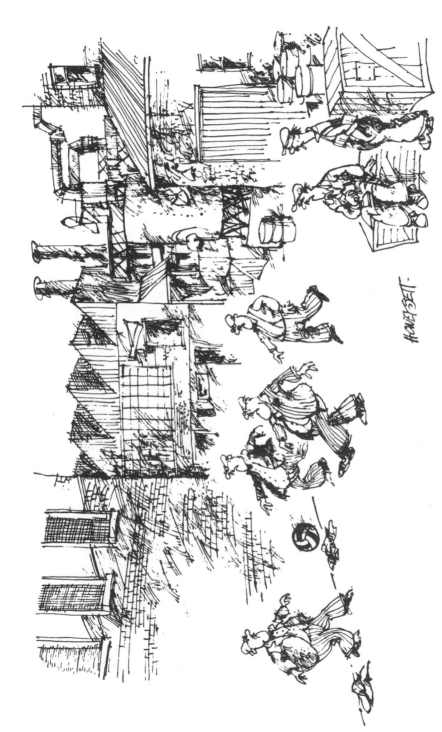

HONEYSETT

"That's what comes of recruiting management from the shop floor."

"Cancelled? . . . the Darts Match?"

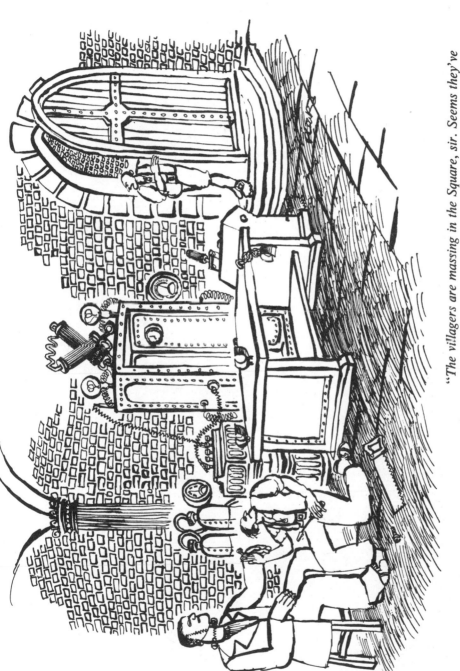

"The villagers are massing in the Square, sir. Seems they've found out that you're not a member of the Affiliated Electrical and Transplant Surgery workers Union."

"You'd think they'd dispense with all those ridiculous formalities at a time like this."

"This is an exhibit — you've already taken the oath."

". . . and it is my case that you, John Hodges, jockey of Newmarket, Suffolk, did . . ."

"This is the wall, Foster. We'd like you to knock up some sort of apt and symbolic mural—you know the sort of thing—The Chairman and Board presiding over the Twin Spirits of Art and Industry as they rise from the Waters of Diligence to reap the rich harvest of Prosperity while the Three Muses, Faith, Hope and Charity flanked by Enterprise and Initiative, bless the Corporation and encourage the shareholders."

"Face facts, man—you're an underprivileged black radical left-wing unemployed person of no fixed address with an Irish accent—of course you're guilty!"

"Now you, sir—you have a question?"

"Look concerned."

"Pardon me, we're from New Orleans—would you call this foggy?"

*"He's lead expectorator in a
punk rock group."*

*"I can fix up your phonograph in a couple of days but we're having a
hell of a job getting hold of the dogs right now."*

"Was there anything else, apart from wanting to sit down for a bit?"

"Monday is out for the break because I have to see my social worker;
Tuesday they're showing a film I wouldn't want to miss; Wednesday's
my pottery lesson . . ."

*"To be honest, I thought I was gate-crashing a
different kind of party."*

*"You're fooling no-one, Henderson, put your clothes on and get back to
work at once."*

"*I wonder how the piccolo player is making out.*"

"*This next song relates my struggle to come to terms with a receding hairline at age twenty-five.*"

Behind the Wheel

"*It keeps him off the streets.*"

"You are now the proud owner of a luxury vehicle, built to the highest standards of this technological age . . ."

"If I can get the old couple out of the boot, I'll give you first refusal."

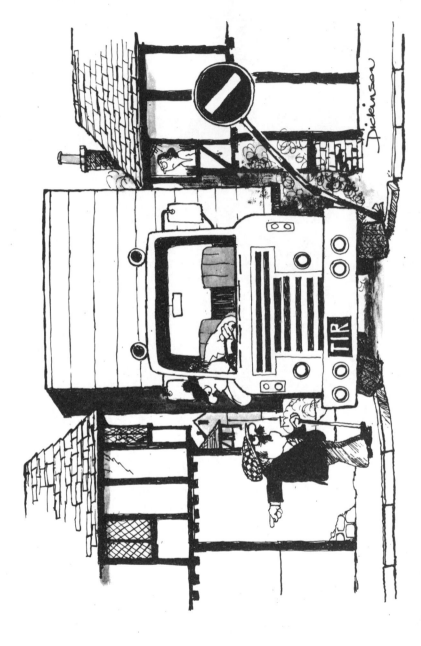

"Smash the next lamp on the left, flatten the pavement by the pub, nudge the sweet shop, scrape the Market Cross, then just follow the skid marks to London."

" Your car will be ready in a couple of weeks, sir. Our senior partner
is personally handling the final series of road tests."

"Keep calm, Mrs. Huxley, but when we get down try to remember exactly what you did."

"'Daily Globe'? There's been a six-vehicle pile up in Maple Road!"

"Don't ring the police! I think it's the one we dumped near St. Albans."

"I find you can always spot the male drivers . . . if they signal left they invariably"

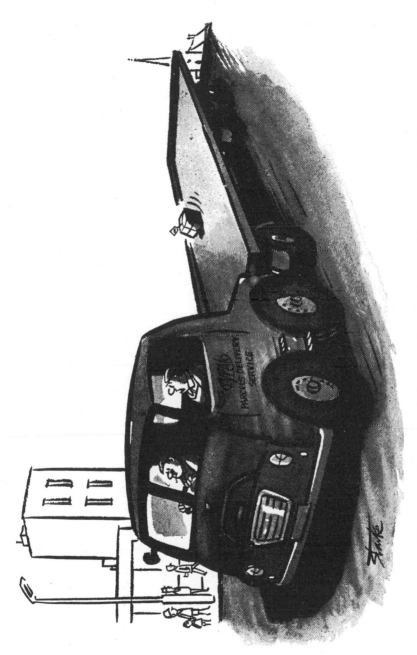

"Step on it, Bert . . . the last one always makes me feel a proper Charlie."

"Sell Surestop Safety Barriers!"

Spiritual Matters

"Where in heaven's name does he get these bizarre 'left wing' notions? 'The meek shall inherit the earth,' indeed!"

"It's the way Angus would've wanted it."

"Don't think I'm unappreciative but I wouldn't mind
holing in two occasionally."

"It was hard bargaining—we get the milk and honey, but the anti-adultery clause stays in."

"Hullo, he's changed his mind about the sling . . ."

"This is most embarrassing to me as a medical man. Apparently I just have to touch them and they're cured!"

"I wonder if it's possible to see him privately."

"I don't think they are ready for the Wheel yet."

"This isn't getting the mission built, Monsignor Perelli . . . ."

"I'm just repeating it to you, you understand. It's really Plato's baby."

"Look—if it's all the same to you, I'm beginning to lose interest in your theory that George Grabbe was the father of Nineteenth Century Romanticism . . ."

Sporting Events

*"An incredible decision by the referee! As I
saw it, it should have been given the other way.*

Still, Mr. Aston is much nearer than I am . . .

. . . so it definitely must have been tails."

"Hello, they're on the defensive—they've reverted to 4-4-2."

HARGREAVES

*"Can't I plead with you, Helen? It isn't my wish that our
marriage should end like this."*

"You really need something to take your mind off your hobby."

"Offer you £50,000 for him . . . £60,000 . . . £70,000 . . . £5,000."

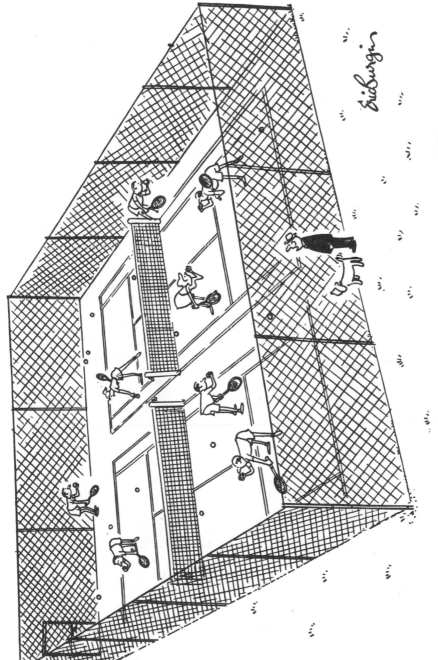

"It's got teethmarks."

The Sex Game

"I think I saw an eyelid flicker."

"Have you got clean underthings? It's your office party today!"

"Can't it wait until tomorrow, Simpson? I've been running behind schedule all day, and I still have to ravish Miss Cooney."

"See anything you fancy?"

"My husband is the kind of man no one notices when he enters a room."

"I don't think the bedroom scenes are very convincing!"

"Can I borrow your mistress tonight?"

*"Funny how times change. They don't laugh any
more when we say we're Mr and Mrs Smith."*

*"Well we **are** trying to be more adventurous,
but we keep having to put on our glasses to
read the manual . . ."*

"Gottle of geer . . . gottle of geer . . ."

"*I wore a topless for two whole weeks on the Costa Brava and didn't get arrested!*"

"*Chicken!*"

"... Oh, come on Paula ...
I'm sure a lot of women
have been mistaken for
Danny la Rue ...!"

KenPyne

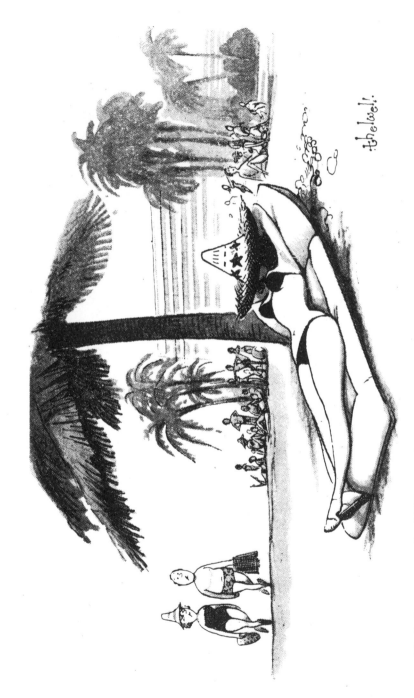

"Isn't that our au pair girl?"

"I just want something to get me from A to B and back without arousing A's suspicions."

"It's so sordid, Charles—having to meet like this."

"It was rather sordid, actually — about a middle-aged husband who comes home at eleven with a rumpled collar and a thin story about working late at the office."

Past and Gone

*Anyway, Abraham begat Isaac; and
Isaac begat Jacob; and Jacob begat
Judas and his brethren; and Judas
begat Phares and Zara of Thamar;
and Phares begat Esrom; and
Esrom begat Aram; and Aram begat
Aminadab; and Aminadab begat
Naasson; and Naasson begat Salmon;
and Salmon begat Booz of Rachab;
and Booz begat Obed of Ruth; and
Obed begat Jesse; and Jesse begat
David the king; David the king
begat Solomon of her that had been
the wife of Urias; and Solomon
begat Roboam; and Roboam begat
Abia; and Abia begat Asa; and Asa
begat Josophat; and Josophat begat
Joram; and Joram begat Ozias; and
Ozias begat Joatham; and Joatham
begat Achaz; and Achaz begat
Ezekias; and Ezekias begat
Manasses; and Manasses begat
Amon; and Amon begat Josias; and
Josias begat Jechonias; and Jechonias
begat Salathiel; and Salathiel begat
Zorobabel; and Zorobabel begat
Abiud; and Abiud begat Eliakim;
and Eliakim begat Azor; and Azor
begat Sadoc; and Sadoc begat
Achim; and Achim begat Eliud; and
Eliud begat Eleazar; and Eleazar
begat Matthan; and Matthan begat
Jacob; and Jacob begat Joseph the
husband of Mary, of whom was born
Jesus. So what's new with you?"*

*"Excuse me! Sorry to bother you. I was
just wondering whether my new
nick-name of 'Bill the Bold' has
caught on yet."*

"... *et tu, Brutus?*"

"*Nothing too ostentatious you understand, Hardy ... make it about 300-odd feet tall and get Landseer to knock up a few lions round the base ...*"

"Go and tell Ahmed that Ramon has been hit, and for God's sake, hurry!"

"Poor Ramon has been hit. You'll have to change the order."

"Make it twenty-six, not twenty-seven."

"We'll have to decide! Are we storming the Winter Palace or the Summer Palace?"

"Thank you. For my next trick I'd like the back six rows to invade Russia."

"It contains health-giving vitamin Jim Smith."

"The rebels have occupied several strongpoints. My men are attacking the cathedral now."

"Gentlemen . . . isolated units of the
enemy have broken through."

"Don't move! You're in the
middle of a minefield!"

*"Gott in Himmel! **Somebody** must have a franc!"*

"Keep your eye on this lot, men. For all we know they may be holding up a completely invisible, new miracle weapon."

"I'm getting a little worried about Olaf."

"Aw c'mon, Genghis—we need one more to make up a horde!"

"I enjoy the inventing. It's laying the rails I hate."

"And before you know they've slammed up another of these modern monstrosities."

"—Quick! Will you marry me?"

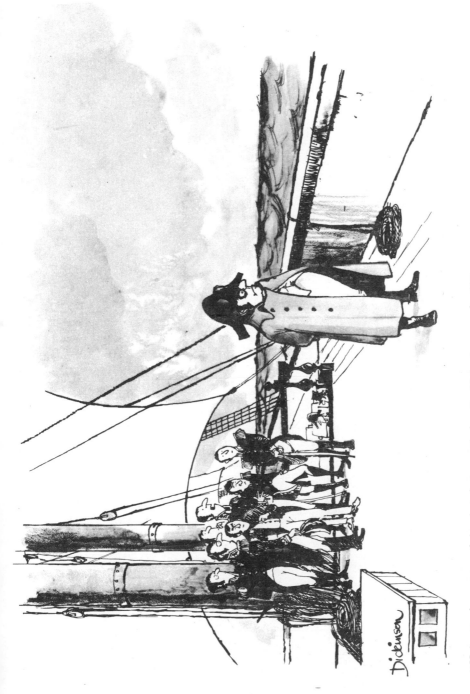

*"He's utterly convinced that he's being exiled to St. **Helen**'s, poor devil!"*

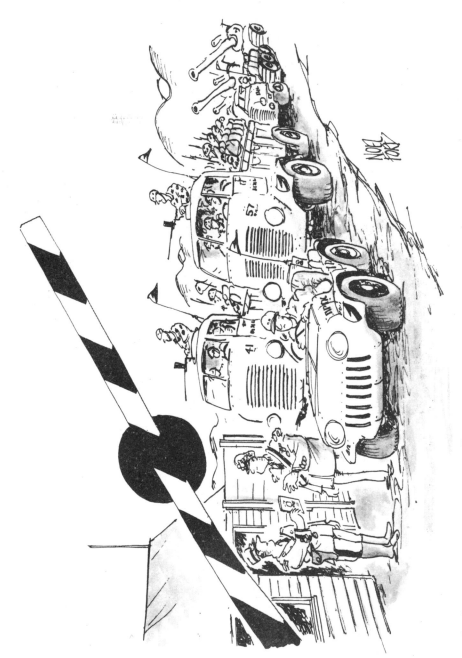

"Thank you, sir. Enjoy your invasion."

Themes and Variations

"Strangely enough, I feel at home here . . ."

"As a matter of fact I've only been here since yesterday—I was appearing in the ship's pantomime."

"That's that then—we've chosen a Prime Minister and a Chancellor of the Exchequer, and we've written to the International Monetary Fund."

"Thank God you finally made it. It's been hell trying to live with Glenn Miller, Amelia Earhart, Adolf Hitler, the Tichbourne claimant and the entire crew of the Marie Celeste."

"On the other hand, we don't charge for the cloud."

"How about this: we move Luke from sailors to medicine, and then give Christopher the travel portfolio . . . ?"

"You passed on three."

"*Business is terrible.*"

"You reached Earth, then?"

"I just shook his hand and he was sick."

"*En français, Jackson, en français.*"

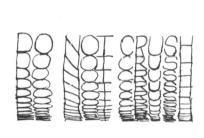

NO SMOK NG

DANG R
E

E. McLACHLAN

"The man we need must have guts, daring and
initiative, Mrs. Hempson! Is your son that man?"

"The man we want is the man with the glint
in his eye. Are you that man?"

Cartoons from PUNCH

"Waste of time, these fire drills."